A LION SCAT AND THREE BLOODY TRACKS IN THE DRIVEWAY

THIS FORM OF SILENCE CALLED *ELLIPSIS OF BATTLE*

AHSAHTA PRESS | BOISE, IDAHO

THE NEW SERIES #89

THE AVALANCHE PATH IN SUMMER

SUSAN TICHY

Ahsahta Press, Boise State University, Boise, Idaho 83725-1580
Cover design by Quemadura
Book design by Janet Holmes
ahsahtapress.org
Copyright © 2019 by Susan Tichy

LIBRARY OF CONGRESS CATALOGING-IN-PUBLICATION DATA

Names: Tichy, Susan, 1952– author.
Title: The avalanche path in summer / Susan Tichy.
Description: Boise, Idaho : Ahsahta Press, [2018] | Series: The new series ;
    #89
Identifiers: LCCN 2018033601 | ISBN 9781934103852 (pbk. : alk. paper) | ISBN
    1934103853 (pbk. : alk. paper)
Classification: LCC PS3570.I26 A6 2018 | DDC 811/.54—dc23
LC record available at https://lccn.loc.gov/2018033601

FOR ALEC FINLAY

AND OTHER MOUNTAIN COMPANIONS

CONTENTS

Looking out from distant
city walls, people see only white clouds.
— WANG WEI,
TR. DAVID HINTON

With mountains, the gap—the irony—that exists between the
imagined and the actual can be wide enough to kill.
— ROBERT MACFARLANE

It requires great effort to annihilate. Therefore we should suspect
that, if we could follow back the history of all negative particles,
we should find that they also are sprung from transitive verbs.
Thus in Chinese the sign meaning "to be lost in the forest" relates
to a state of non-existence. English "not" = the Sanskrit na . . .
may come from the root na, *to be lost, to perish.*
— ERNEST FENOLLOSA

Where rending is the law of being, it is the law of loveliness.
— JOHN RUSKIN

BECAUSE IT WAS A MOUNTAIN

ROUTE SKETCHED ON A MAP, AS IF WALKING

were a kind of drawing, large-scale,
repeatable. Yet, like the body, a walk
exists only as it happens. Look back,
if you can, and call the telling
a literature of paradise: the long days,
the short nights, wrapped up in an army poncho,
rolled in under the willow-brush to sleep, while
'at every moment some new ridge
seemed to start into existence.' Now
double the silence by listening to it:
some old tide-race nothing now
but a seep with yellow warblers. From there,
you may darken the way with a pencil,
steepen the avalanche path in accord
with leg muscles that hurt for days—
the *near* retaining evidence
of *far*. You may say, if you wish,
it was 'quite monotonous all the way up,
composed of a winding tendril'—
though not if you copy accurately
those seventeen spruce cut off
at the depth of snow, their scattered trunks
awash in a lake of flowers: the scene
of force in all its glory. Nothing else known
if it cannot be measured in strides—
and no two equal. That is why
you must 'tenderly unite the darker tints,'
devote the day to surviving the mountain
(that's meant to say *surveying*, sorry)—

a mingling of topography and math,
or footsteps with quotations. Genre may be
a pleasant ramble or 'stumbling, groaning,
slipping and pulling up short, over stones,
puddles, snow-wet grass, and every variety of pitfall,
including cows.' So tell me again
about the fall through ice, and I'll tell you
of my boots on the trail, a well-drawn fact
despite the 'solitude of frozen peaks.'
For after paradise comes the body,
with 'all its goddamn ups and downs—'
its *night frost has hardened the snow*, or
soak a kitchen towel in a bowl of tea,
lay it over a sunburned back. Take in
the undulating *near*, the *far* level,
blue and cold, with 'terraces of pure velvet'
(otherwise known as evening shadows),
clouds on the move ('like weeds
in a river current'), and a dozen moraines
thrown about in a kind of frenzy.
I remember it all, the view was splendid,
and I've marked the spot where,
'struggling to remember
where she put her foot on the way up,'
the dog crawled into my rucksack to sleep.

ALIVE

Words—not much use here
So walk straight into that, the trap
Of sunlight, three spare thrushes
Alive in the underbrush

And if 'by being alive to difficulty
One can avoid it,' I'll take all night
To pack one pack, clean one boot
A first embellishment, last correction, and

'What strange things we are'—the thrushes'
Voices, explainable, by split syrinx
Doubling song, so it seems to arrive
From two directions, now try to find them

In wrist-thick vines, in pine-duff hush:
Sublime, awful, dreadful, grand
Longinus' words for *affect* reassigned
To mist and rock, to distance and

'It's the quietness of the danger
I love,' the pre-dawn light
On snowy ridges, cup-rings on the map
A solid wall

Of steep dark spruce and a snow-chute
That tumbles into young aspen
Water-greedy, pale as moths: puddle mirror
On a flat rock, what will I see?

'Expendable man where horrid crag'
Or 'transferring my winged thoughts'
Fault line where a world ends/
Begins, governed by laws of a wholly

Other existence, up-to-date explanations
Of avalanches, and—
'He shot the radio and then himself'
So says my radio, but 'you must

Go on, again with the pen'
The body, like all conspirators
Untrustworthy, driven like cloud
From steep to steep, or

Narrow wet trail through head-high
Willows—a rough paper, a pencil line—
A painter whose brush technique was called
'The capture of a fort in war' or

'Decreasing resemblance to anything'
Yet each fact verifiable—
'Demand for mountain epiphanies' and
Why that boulder lies in that field

Exact words as I wrote them down
Thrush, thrush, thrush, thrush
One teaspoon of snow unmelted
On the shadow side of a rock

'A TREE AT ITS BIRTHPLACE,
A BOULDER AT ITS RESTING PLACE'

Boots and a walking stick: young again
Rucksack and spine one body
With violets on a mountain path
High-snow-scent in the wind—
Stoop to count bracts, straighten to view

The ten thousand things: summer flowers
Bent to the shape of the stream
Threads of snowmelt down rock-faces
Thin, then broaden, quicken the river:
Ten-year trees in the avalanche path—

They measure the length
Of drought—a facing slope
Of tall, dark spruce, threaded with ghostly
Purple: dead trees, drought-killed:
Violets on a mountain path

Look up at the headwall:
Rock pillars breaking, the breaking
Now scree underfoot, so feel your way
Stumble through waist-high bluebells
To the boulder, split   as if by lightning

And the tree's bare bark—branches above
Branches below—a three-foot gap where an avalanche
Ripped over head-deep, hard-packed snow, the source
Of bluebell, gromwell, houndstongue, horsemint
Nodding onion, blue-eyed grass

Bistort, sorrel, and death camas
Sandwort and chickweed, elephant head
(with marsh marigold, past its prime)
Rosecrown, kingscrown, vetch and lupine
Parry primrose, shooting star—the wind

Here seems to carry light, as in this long ellipsis
The battle remains visible: force of snow
Force of sun, unstoppable as
A bull-elk leaping down the tundra
Fluted Peak, thirty years ago

Bending—when he saw us—farther west
Then down and gone, so near his musk
Can wake me, now, from dream

BECAUSE IT WAS A MOUNTAIN WHERE I FELL

Palm-path-pain
step-stop-stipple

land-roll   headwall
bone   ballast

pain-as-ghost
in the cloud-clear-cloud

Which is self
Which is world

ANOTHER HAUNTING, THE PENCIL LINE

that shimmers under paint, goes on
into the raw paper : the way
imagined but never walked : a shape
                    of ridge and stormcloud,
                    ridge and scree,
the hand alone descending
to paper's edge : the melancholy
                    endless what-ifs
of Ruskin's unfinished drawings :
curve of a snow-chute,
match-stick pine trunks
        fallen   or flung :
'the most magnificent piece of ruin
I have yet seen'
        or beds of limestone   bent like a rainbow
                    ('a fine accomplice to metaphysics')
                    ('erodes according to first flaws')
: pockets of detail, unsurrounded,
like stones from a tricklet—
red pebble the size of two match heads
laid on paper, traced in lead,
        the tracings caught
in same vortex, sprindrift
haunting the highest ridges.
        And where in this body
is pain to be found? Down here,
in too-dense, drought-wrought forest
dead spruce lean, but can't fall :
the way imagined but never walked,
or never walked again.

AT A ROCKSLIDE ENDING IN WILLOW
A LARKSPUR TALLER THAN WILLOW

Not *taller than willow*
but telling the sparrow

Not *telling the sparrow*
but *not shy*

at eye-level—
sings, flits, sun

on the willow-wave
wind-

driven flies
on the snow, the snow

calicoed
by rock-dust, algae, red

as a kestrel's tail
Step

through its trickling edge
'breaking the colours

amongst each other'
What's there to be seen

What's seen

'A WALK IS FACT FOR THE WALKER
AND FICTION FOR EVERYONE ELSE'

Sunrise on the snowfields
Storm cloud snagged on a near point
The high pastures, deep in flowers
'Torrents plunging through cloven ravines'

Or an easy shelf-trail, soft footing
Young oak, rain-wet, in a shaft of sun
Only mist on the move, deadfall on the slopes
One fragment of snow remaining

Say *fluid geometry of hills*
Momentarily stilled, say
One dead pine, rose-colored
Or a calculated hyperbole of rock

Feel free to wander within the poem
Separate perceptions into points of view
Complete a sentence, divide a rhyme
Yet facts remain—

'New clouds born over high, bare rock'
'Moonlight shining through open gates'
Assent in words
That nothing can be expressed in words

Dipped boots in mud and walked the distance
In a spiral on the gallery floor

POCKETS OF DETAIL, UNSURROUNDED
(A BEAR CIRCLED OUR CAMP ALL NIGHT)

Rain filtered through rock
Re-emerging from rock
With trees dwarfed, splayed—
A stumble, then, a twisting
Thought—'as the body may be said

To think'—singing all night
Off-key, to calm my horse
Other horse tangled up in a picket rope
—she always does that, silly girl—
For a mountain can take you

Out of yourself, or *in*
Remember that day
The three of us going single-file
As we turned along the shelf-trail
Joined by a fourth—a bighorn ram

Trailing us out of his territory
Like an usher seeing
Unruly guests to the door
Pseudo-narcissus, narcissus, they grow
So close together above that trail

TO SPEAK OF ONE IS TO SPEAK OF THE OTHER

Live trees mourn the dead ones, feed their roots
for years : thin flanks

of a worn-out doe, her twins
won't make it, either

'And I did not weary myself in wishing
that a daisy could see the beauty of its shadow'

ON THE TRAIL, A WOMAN STOPS TO ASK ME WHY I AM NOT AFRAID

Star-grass blooming in the real grass.
Marmot whistles mistaken for birds.
Keep war and ruin *a distant thunder*,
Not *young bear standing on a bloated cow*—
What a word can, and cannot, do.

So, that smell of meat where the caterpillars
Having eaten the aspen moved on to willow
And now lie rotting in the rain puddles—is that
'A hunger for willed and authentic fear,' or
Doubled darkness, be sincere?

Through bare trees, you can see the mountain.
From the mountain you see
A rock or two, some broken branches,
The path through empty and full.
'So pleased I trembled' : an artifice

Of scooped corries, u-shaped valleys
Gigantic boulders and blade-like ridge :
Suspended force of omitted words, of
Cliffs the gate, pines the path, of
'Granite slops about like porridge,

Basalt bubbles like stew.'
And a smudge of rock-smoke
When you break one open, that
Steady burgeoning forth of *things*.
Step then step, image then image.
Star-river poised like a sword above my roof.

NOT LOST, EXACTLY

Crouched at the top of an old rockslide, red
and mixed-up, Permian boulders pinned to the slope
by bristlecone, sandwort, asters, stonecrop :
looking for snow but it's August, snowbanks gone away
like a hermit monk—found in the not-finding—

cinquefoil in bloom, cuddled up to a silver, wind-shorn log,
driftwood/windwood, barbed wire threading
through stands of lupine—they used to run cattle up here—
two juncos palling around with a bluebird
(all of them kids and a bit confused)—go

boulder-hopping through bristlecones—
too high for pain, high on the silvery
trunks of the long-dead, the lightning-bolted
the sheer amaze of a slick-shine uplifted rock-face
water-blackened—*from death in valleys*

preserve me, o lord—harebells and pussy toes
leathery leaves of kinnikinnick
and what Macfarlane calls *delusion*, belief
that you might come to know a place completely
exactly *because* of its boundlessness, its

avalanche lilies along the stream, its
throw me a line and I can respond
in kind : a bird's nest in a deer's ribcage
(wren? chickadee? couldn't be raven)
its wind-history, its ant-map, the charm

of a bare midriff/mid-drift   on a sapling spruce :
a kind of navigation that looks
like sun-and-cloud-shadow over twenty peaks—
not lost, exactly, just headed downhill
on the wrong used-to-be-a-road

of pinball gravel, felled trees, loose rock
and the bulldozed humps that keep
motorbikes at bay, arcing
the wrong way down the mountain
to spill out I-don't-know-where

but not at the place I parked the truck.
So, low on water, cutting cross-slope
on a game-trail, following instructions
from the Dao—translated, sometimes
as Way-making—that *knowing, seeing,* and *doing*

do not exist apart from *local,* apart from
know-how, know-what, know-whence
know water-bar and scolding squirrel
know rock-time, log-ache, pebble-mouth
and how to look back—just now and then—

so that, returning, you'll know the way
even though—yeah yeah, blah blah, I know—
the Way's been in ruins a thousand years
and one wrong road is as good
as any other.

IN THE 15TH CHAPTER ON INFINITY,
TRY TO ARREST ONE DETAIL

A cobble of quartz in cemented silt, perhaps,
or moss campion—what Nan Shepherd called
'the clumps of silence.' For 'the touch of a pen
lends great transparency to shadows'
—that's Ruskin, who helped us see mountains
move. *You look as if you'd seen a ghost,*
somebody said, as I tried to count waves
in a cliff face, the perfectly transparent story
of a fault-block uplift range, two to three miles
above sea-level. A fault-block uplift range, that is,
from which the first three billion years of earth history
are missing. 'Wield the brush lightly'
is good advice, for 'colour must not
be dragged about and disturbed.' Where color
has been dragged about (otherwise known
as a *thrust fault* in sedimentary rock)
a confusion of pebbles, cobbles, clasts,
bound each to each, in a matrix of gravel,
all fed on water : all fed on water, then broken up,
up-lifted, inter-tongued, and 'the quicker
a line is drawn, the lighter it is at the ends,'
meaning: 'more easily joined with other lines,'
more easily joined as rippling beds,
rainbowed purple, gray, blue—that high, wavy rock
on Crestone Peak, or vertical caves
above the Swift Creek crossing—
reduced, on a map, to heavy black lines
with teeth pointing upward, toward the thrust
of what geologists call *a hanging wall.*

On what geologists call *a hanging wall*
what appears to be pointed is always curved,
with lines of escape for rock, water, cloud.
Lines of escape means 'talus everywhere—
world of grief!' Believe it when it's underfoot,
or found in an old field-notebook : my handwriting,
Ruskin's words : all *distant* colour
is *pure* colour, any failure there 'will at once do away
with all remoteness.' A terrible price:
to begin with Nan Shepherd's 'hummocky snow
—or was it sea?'—rise to the level
of 'pure and terrible streams,' wind up
with sun-on-snow-means-a-sunburned-throat.
'When care is at fault,' Ruskin replies,
'a little carelessness will help . . . '
but chance will not help us with the mountain,
its 'fine and faintly organized edge,'
its families of ridges, its sweet moraines—
'entirely composed of heaps of stones—'
where at times you catch below your feet
a glint of water, a trace. 'Water has no darkness,'
Shepherd says, not even in 'its most appalling quality,'
its strength. Not even when it fingers down
a dark hornblende—gabbro to gneiss—
a green-black metamorphic, rising
in a headwall the size of a city . . . skirted
with muscovite, chlorite, epidote : green
and more green : pebbles and cobbles
among gray granite, rose quartz, and a pale tonalite

thrust to the very top of a peak. There is no poem here
called *Lines of Rest*, no exercise labeled
hill color. Just bullying winds, and a list of facts:
the wreckage of ancestral mountains, where
'light and a state of being are facts.'

'Slaty crystallines, slaty coherents—
is this not marvelous?' Ruskin declared
of a world built on propositions.
'One is *companioned*, though not in time,'
she wrote of tracks, and rocks. And once:
'peering into a lake, I thought it shallow
because I could see its depths.'

AND, JUST FOR THE RECORD, I'D LIKE TO SAY THAT I CAN'T DO WHAT I JUST DID

Fourteen miles, and the day short

Half the time couldn't carry my own pack

What an old man of a woman I am

But 'paths, once walked, create sinew'

And 'though I straddle my horse, there is no way back'

Become that trail   its bark, its rock

Sip tea   from 'the strong, white water of rivers'

'NOT BY SCALE BUT BY AGGREGATION'

Lock the truck hubs before you need them
When in doubt, steer high
Coming or going, leave a stone at the grotto
If you don't have a stone, leave hair
Carry dry socks, your headlamp
pen and paper in a leg pocket
Don't pitch your tent on fresh hail
If you find a tree trunk in a meadow
look for the root-hole half a mile up-hill
Chew up a willow leaf, stick it on a bee sting
Be sure to re-visit your favorite rocks
Chopsticks are lighter than forks
Caught out by lightning—squat, don't sit
Criss-cross your verbs, like little game-trails in the willow
Hang on to your hat
The leaf of wild geranium looks pretty much like monkshood
—don't harvest till it blooms
A bighorn knows the difference between walking stick and gun
Take care of your maps
Where you crossed dry-footed in August
you'll have to wade in June
If you can't pick your feet up, you stumble
If you stumble twice, it means your back is tired
Walk in old riverbeds
Kick loose rocks off the trail
Do not praise most what you think fewest people have seen
Bears, too, are fond of flowers
Watch for gray jays—they're shy

LONG WALK AFTER TOO LITTLE SLEEP

Wet camp, rock tea
'each leaf cut

by a fingernail'
yesterday's clothes

dripping
from the trees

'Look for masters
find paths'

says Wang Wei
—or did I write that

in the trail guide?
River beds tangle

on their way downhill
some hold water

some hold trees
the path between cliffs

narrow here
a snow-fed river

colder than air

Mist rides it
face-high, ghosty

No fossils here
but deer tracks

lead to firmer sand
'To expel the froth

that carries bitterness'
'to make the water

spill over the pot'
—bistort

in the water-meadow
Cloud-come-to-earth

's what I would call it
(wet boots

and a rill to walk through)
flycatcher dodging

my eyes in the dripping
willow
        Then rock

so climb it—
patchwork of aspen

rock-slab, spruce
on the north slope

facing scree
Goshawk glides down

in the wind
shadow

crosses the path

of the avalanche
                    (mist

tumbling down
the headwall

shreds head-high
in the headless

trees)
        'Nothing brighter

than white paper
nothing blacker

than wet ink'
——meaning

that everything is
Bighorn scat

on the quartzy
glitter

a slight redaction
'unchecked ruin'

of Ruskin's treatise
on mountain light

——'though the hand may stagger
a little'

wielding the brush-tip
testing the pitch

of basement rock
slick when wet

and the newer trace
of an old roadbed

perfectly clear
from a distance

Smell of wet rock
skirting wet rock

(finch on the old snow
picking up flies)

and a granite taste
in the air
                              Tea

from a thermos—
white breath—

'at a point from which
one might turn back'

buttercup riding
the toe of my boot

boot leather scarred
by a stumble

wild parsley, chiming bells (the knee-high kind)
a bit of yarrow, a shooting star, a raft of death camas
if you dare look down—hang on to the trees—
then drop to the streambed, keeping one hand
on the rock-face, step over, or through,
that clear pool at water's edge
to stone steps with wet boots—slippery—
up to a comfy moraine, a favorite boulder, spot of sunshine
in dense trees above the spate, a spate
bringing snow-melt down from the cirques and tarns :
moving water to a mountain
as pollen to a flower, says Nan Shepherd, and then
'if I had other senses, there are other things
I should know' : think year-year,
wood-window, waking at dawn,
both legs so full of memory : June-high water
at the end of July : no crossing,
and *there*—a ten-inch brook trout
body-surfing the white water :
no, that's a rare sort of green-backed
cut-throat—somebody told us after the fact—
wood-nymphs and spotted saxifrage
dotting the slope where you start up onto
that narrow, side-hill, excuse for a trail :
what a laugh, the ravens   quoting Ruskin :
their black feathers   the white light :

AFTER PARADISE

If *horse from the borderland* means gray
white-crowned sparrow song means high
and climbing into such views means pure

confusion—

T'ao Ch'ien was certain: 'the path of high peaks
never falters' : schist : rain : bowing
a thousand years into moving water

Look across Sand Creek to the snow-chutes—
one sharp/short run of rock
then baby spruce in a patch of willow

waterfalls in the dark-slash gullies
knifed by snow-melt, wrecked
by sun : three elk silhouette

on a scrap of snowfield
oceans of half-dead trees around them :
budworm : wildfire : everything

in abundance—

SMALL VOLCANO OF A MUSHROOM, PUSHING THROUGH SOIL

So, what's the quarry? summit?
one-sided wintergreen?

or rough descent on rock and moss
to a good spot for drinking tea?

Stand on a boulder at creekside:
point with your stick to a bog orchid

one boot on a wine-red vein   of silt
driven through sweeps of coarser sand:

cross-grained, flecked   with mica—sunlight
a few million years from its birth

Summit photo: entirely cloud
Vireo in the aspen: silent   but clear

I have other lives
but do not know how to exist

without this one

CERTAINTY

'IN COUNTRY THAT IS ROUGH, BUT NOT DIFFICULT,
ONE SEES WHERE ONE IS AND WHERE ONE IS GOING
AT THE SAME TIME'

As rock speaks to any
trained or curious eye :

someone else
sometime else

laid down words—
thin sheets or thick—

something broke them
lifted, pressed them

here : each rippled sand
each pebble clenched :

motion rendered
visible, in red boulders

thick with clasts, a wild
conglomerate, something made

of other things where
'pain and suffering shape

the mind,' a quite implausible
'up above' where wind hammers

worlds together : *convenient*
and *bleak*

reduced to *brash* or
lichen crust as brute matter

wind/light/space
a mystery thick

as contour lines on an old map
—called *reticent*

or maybe *clitched,* or
'looking back down

the path to the sea'
—I meant *seabed*

a fossil storm just
part way up

to *paradise*—look here :
a shallow dip in rough scree

'where water comes gradually
into focus' only because

it trembles : that is wind
speaking softly

heard by those who carry pain
as others carry

talismans, a *descendental*
willingness

to walk all day in pursuit
of fear—I mean

to corner it, trap it, parse it
thumbing a rock

of green/black waves
touching light

in the form of leaf
time in a metamorphic

stone : 'and who
with any sense

can't be interested
in *that*?'—the sheen

the shades, the *Gates*
of Delirium—

sandstone, sandwort
iron oxide

thought or spasm
touch or word :

where a breeze
crosses pain flutters

muscle, ligament
sediment, sentiment

trees bent flat
by wind and snow

skirling waves
of rock uplifting :

try to stand there
try to find

a *there* exactly
touching *here*

a timberline
so crystal clear

so free of pity
free of dread

and all the lakes
that live there still

as wind

Clouds roll eastward, white and high
then quick and gray
so pause here on an easy trail
to rub bare shoulders through white fir
then neck, face, halfway between
a furry pelt and a wing of feathers :
sensation caught like a single pebble
snatched on the journey from mud to shale
shale to schist : just try
to make of pain an offering
laid at the shrine of upright walking :
not 'beds laid down in quiet waters'
but the sorting, reworking, of ever-motion
pebbly sands of a braided stream
or a handful of metamorphosis :
this rock carried from the cabin yard
to leave in a lightning-shattered tree
shrine to danger, shrine to time
in which dark veins are pure :
the bleed is rosy, invades host rock
—or so says the geologue
of fracture, of fault, of a body's
internal thrashing :
crystal by crystal, grain by grain
Now quick! look up! a single raven
—then four more—skying southward, all talking
of something local, something urgent : what?

'THE ONE THAT FEEDS IT AND THE ONE THAT DRAINS IT SHOW AS WHITE THREADS ON THE MOUNTAIN'

Immune to time, that meadow

where my horse, ten years dead
pulls back his tender lips

to nip purple thistle

Wildfire smoke
drifts over a distant glitter

And fallen water is in the hands of water

OF HALF THE VIEWS I HAVE YET SAID NOTHING

of wind to bully a waterfall
back up the cliff.

of black and white butterflies
hail on dust / no rain

in deadfall timber
two or three miles that feel like eight

of stepping over
torn and blistered

(wild rose petals
on the toe of my boot)

the creek, when we reach it
dry / and wrong

the map in our heads
—torn at an old crease—

useless now :
we turn downhill

At the foot of the range
a river of yellow

pours
through blackened trees

(flowers chest-high
boots ash-covered)

'Before us lie
the wild targets'

wrote Du Fu
wrote

stone-skin-broken
startle-heart

Deer tracks will lead us
to firmer ground

and time passes
—don't worry boys—

riverbeds in pillars
at the Customs House

'TO HAVE PAIN IS TO HAVE CERTAINTY,
TO HEAR OF PAIN IS TO HAVE DOUBT'

From a high ridge, what Ruskin called
'the mystery of clearness itself,'
a grammar in which *between* means *world*,
among means overlapping planes
of wind, bark, cloud, flowers, rock,

or sitting in stillness, meditation shaped
like a mountain. *And what does it feel like?*
Feels : like a tide-race of gravel
driven though mud, the whole shenanigan tilted
up and broken down.

'But iron is only in the black rock'
says Ruskin, the rock-man. 'And
falls very prettily,' says Ruskin, the art-.
'Called Alpine for distinction's sake—'
shank, thighbone, outermost limb,

all so 'naked, terrible, and rent.'
White cliffs, like glaciers, break the green :
believe it when it's underfoot :
a limestone holding snails, sea lilies
(list of expenses follows the list of rocks), all

storybook-clear, with a stack of basalt
'broken, alas, in youth.' —What's this, some code
for wind-drunk, for rain-staggered,
for one foot caught and a whipcrack
up the spine? *To ask* means

to balance : large-small, long-short, heavy-light.
And the answer means not *horse-sudden*,
more like a thousand miles of smoke and fire.
Means year-year, wood-window, opening
in a place where *nothing* comes, where

lost-in-the-woods, where earth-endure.
From there you can hear *vulture* rise
from *use-mouth, carve*—or *stem segments
of a sea lily*. What do you see?
A distant white in the rock-face, sand

in the tire tracks, evidence
of 'frost and spate and drought,'
a horseshoe cirque for Horseshoe Lake,
ruffle of spruce at the rim. Past full, the moon
looks grass-boundless, no-rain sky,

and a thousand gates opening, one by one.
Yet, careful, careful :
hand-snatch-from-moon means
to have, to be, does not mean *see*,
does not mean doubt

must necessarily follow from
the well-known silence of rock.
Ruskin, the curious, had no need
to draw what could be easily seen.
Bird-fly can mean *repeat, repeat,*

or *distance* or merely *water runs clear*
at the rough, far-out ends of things.
Not for the eye, and not for nothing
did Keats write, of his only hike
'I will clamour through clouds and exist.'

if not believed, and I have better ghosts
than this one—less fictive, more convincing—
though *stigmatized* and *valorized*
are dialectally connected :
narratives of the turning point :
stopping to rest at a switchback
or *forcing the truck up stair-step rock*
the management   and mangling
of small genres, tall tales :
'the unhelpful doctor'   'the steep part'
and telling, I'm told, can be dangerous
anything typed can be stolen, misread
is panic the proper response to this
avalanche is a verb, *wildfire* is a fact
is panic the proper response
to eighty miles of dead trees
is panic the proper response
to a place in the body that will not heal
or a place ~~in the body~~ that will not heal
always longer and always higher
where does this start and the mountain end
built up in layers, year by year
fused by water and increments
of stone : gravel pinched between thin sheets
or is it metamorphic   is it the name of a flower
define *seclusion*   define *incarceration*
what the doctor calls *catastrophic thinking*
a distance measured but never crossed
my friend says 'if you don't love it

44

it's gone'   young siskin lies in the cabin's
shadow, half-eaten, hollowed by ants
if I say half-eaten by chipmunks
does the poem become comedy   is comedy true
beating my fist on my leg means
mouth closed, not crying out
beating my fist on my leg means
bearing what is expected to pass
thesis / antithesis : I have conquered
nothing / nothing cannot be conquered
truth and *secret* so easily joined
fossil feathers brush my hand
and the doctor says try   to be *interested*
the nurse mixing a cocktail of drugs
my body is expected to hold
does repetition make story a lie
does pain make every story a lie :
crouched down under a rain poncho
sweat-wet tee-shirt, shorts and boots
hugging my big, wet, terrified dog
pummeled by rain, then hail
my hat covered in aspen leaves
the temperature dropping
forty degrees in as many minutes
now *that's* a story   tellable
and true   more palpable
than bloody urine splashing on rock
it's happened before, it comes, it passes
it's happened before but not here

would I even know   and what would I know
had I been squatting on red rock
I was not alone in the hailstorm
I am always alone at the end of a question
are there enough drugs in my pocket
are there enough drugs in the world
white-crowned sparrow sings in the willow
(that's *willow-brush*, not *willow-tree*)
on a scale of one to ten :
uncountable rills from snow to stream
on a scale of one to ten :
two steep ridges cupping the trail
six miles from the truck and a risen moon
on a scale of one to ten :
eight years seven months and counting
therapist says *try   to be interested*
physical therapist says
go out in the morning, walk till it hurts
then come back and show me
the broken flowers, eight inches of hail
a poor-will calling, nothing remains
of that dog but bones—panic-grass they call it—
doesn't grow here—tell yourself—
as you walk down, as you walk down
as you enter the windowless room

'WITHOUT EXAGGERATION, WITHOUT MYSTERY, WITHOUT ENMITY, & WITHOUT MERCY'

In a wet year, June: a family of dippers
in Huérfano Road:

river up to the truck's hubcaps

In a dry year, June: that popcorn smell of scorched grass
under a car's hot belly:

last year's grass

View from the trail, here, now: a thousand square miles
of what woodcutters call

dead standing

stark as the eyes of a sick doe, shot at the foot of my cabin steps:
before the blood jet, that look

of mere surprise

EVERY STEP STUBBORN

on a whiplash path
rockfall rain :

pump blood and lymph
through muscle, fascia

joints of the sacrum
nested, not fused

so the slightest twist
of fall, whip-

crack of spine and tailbone bends
stumbles   revises itself :

new boots, new pack
ice-heat-massage, and still

piss tells a story any mammal
not human can read—

splashed on rose-quartz trapped in mudstone
mica as slick   as a buttercup leaf :

boot knows the difference, finger points
and a cup leaves rings on the map

claims territory where there had been none
I mean, of course, 'those things within range

of human thought' : acts of enclosure
invention of trespass, of metaphor

'the struck-match odor of split rock'
'and it starts to move with a dreadful sound

a molar grating in your jaw
as the dentist works to extract it'—

the hip, the pelvis   loosening
on slopes so steep you can smell the flowers

without stooping
without stopping

the long, smooth *up*, or a ragged climb
you know must be descended

At the upper crossing, a colder wind
high-water that yesterday was snow

Piss where a dipper
watches me watching

Not all ranges, not all things

'In the fluid surge sucked out of you
by sensing   that there is no other Way'

DAYS GROW SHORTER, BUT THE TRAILS DO NOT

Six hours up, two at timberline :
linger long
in the cirque of golden willow

then three hours down :
meet bow-hunters in the yellow trees—
blackened faces, camo, smiles

Yes, we're local, yes the lakes
and yes the trail   six miles, the steep
the easy, yes   But no

we've seen no elk, no deer, no war
a bear perhaps, or maybe not—
the trees were thick, we heard, we think—

Sit for a while at the upper crossing
gaze at tundra, red   as summer deer
In a poem this means

snow in hair or *friends soon part*—
'Meanwhile / the image
is / as it does'

my friend writes   in the book of pain :
laughter and headlamps
answer the rising moon

'SEA FOAM, FOR INSTANCE, CANNOT BE DRAWN AT ALL' [A TRACT OF SOLITUDE & SAVAGENESS]

In the darknesses, as Ruskin says
        (windhorse, woodstove, tin cup, rake)
Perfection of *unclarity*—
'A bank of grass with all its blades
Or a bush with all its leaves'
Wildfire ash falls on the roof
Masked like a bandit, I sweep the steps
        (square nails, hammer, a fawn's leg bone
        retrieved from a lion-kill)
New neighbors call the crows *ravens*, the ravens *hawks*
Doctor wants me to describe the pain
        (pill bottles, bird bath
        scribbled evacuation list)
Three vultures over my roof, three *eagles* over theirs
The body breathes and the book says
Try to feel your feet on the floor
        (floorboard, go-bag, pocket knife, shrike)
When I am silent she offers words
When I shake my head she types *patient refuses*
        (hand-made table, hand-made bench
        weasel, coyote, firewood, truck)
That I was there cannot be unsaid
        (hand-pump, deep well, hard water)
Ruskin says: 'Now, if you can draw that stone
You can draw anything'
Doctor says: if you change the way you walk
        (*clast* from the Greek   *klastos* : broken)
'I mean, anything that can be drawn'

                 (old mud dried on old boots
                 new spider web at the cabin door)
Practice walking, that's what she said
Walk no farther than the gate
                 (work-gloves, work-boots, pruning saw)
Wind turns pages in the open book
I could have typed *oracle book*
                 (bird in the house, mid-day sun
                 young buck sleeping under the porch)
Birds come and go, pain comes and goes
'And the worst can be relieved by swearing—'
I could have sworn she said that
Though what I remember is often wrong
                 (ash-bucket, water-bucket
                 metal skirting, moat of rock)
And right action, Ruskin says,
Can only proceed from right seeing
                 (miner's candle, shooting star
                 the cystoscope on its long neck)
Doctor says I must change the way I walk
                 (as one by one each drop of blood
                 forms   and falls in the deepest ranges)
That I had these thoughts cannot be proven
That a single step was laid, erased
That I watched the blood, that I turned away
That I praised the gate as if it were a mountain
                 (hung like a mask on the cabin wall
                 the hard, dry pelvic bone of a deer)

BLUE TIN CUP

Attack or rescue, the throb of a helicopter
passes westward over the road, kicks my heartbeat
up to the speed of sound. 'Murderous furnace
of non-being' : red-tail hawk in an intersection,
crouched, hissing, over a flattened rabbit.
Attack or rescue : skew the truck and stop
to shield the bird. Watch the chopper
cut southwest to the line of high peaks, high temple
to a pure and terrible danger : that red conglomerate—
sweet to a dry boot, treacherous wet.
                    Treacherous wet, that's true,
but the day he fell the rock was dry, was fine,
was don't know what—no aiming sticks
or range-finders blooming among the harebells.
So skew the truck, watch the chopper,
save his statue of Guanyin from the fire :
his Guanyin, his Bronze Star,
his walking stick and the truck and tent—
all saved from the fire, a vagrant fire
that stopped a mile from the cabin steps.
'Sports of Nature in a whimsical mood—'
called rocks and mountains, trees and wind : wind.
'And where the trickles of water crossed it—'
and wherever the trickles of water crossed it—
                    Come back to yourself. The chopper's gone.
The chopper's gone and your boots are wet
among the vetch and yarrow. No two crossings
taste the same—snowmelt, tannin, granite, flood.
Fill the blue tin cup with water.
Swallow its shocking cold.

AT THE MOUNTAIN WHERE HE FELL

As a rock balanced on pillar of ice
As pebbles dislodged in a single step

And much to learn
of walk-road   mouth-sound   deer-dust   silt

bone-blade as the root
of *separation*

Wing beat : to repeat, to practice
Grass-road   bird-door   stone sky

LOST

'Call on Heaven in the wild grasses—'
a river of aspen—leafless, white—

falls through steep, dark pine
on the canyon wall : take that route

or 'up the moraine toward China'   listen
for 'the musketry of rockfall

the bomb-rumble   of avalanche'—
but this is autumn, only last year's snow

clinging like moss on the highest rock
then pelting rain, gray-lit

and the birds silent :
thunderhead thirty-thousand feet

but twenty miles off :   sun slants through rain
onto rock-gray summits

they look like dream
or prison walls, they look like fear

So walk the fear out of your dreams
walk the war out of your fear

with fear of height, of looking down
a thousand-foot drop   to water

Flowers drop tears, birds carry thought
toward distant light—a growing-green

and a stone-green—half-translated
or not at all : compression of word

compassion of snow
companion of rock from summit to sea

sea to summit : walk only as far
as timberline lakes, the border between

what's soft, what's sere :
where water tastes like tannin, like leaf

willow brush so dense the path
is theoretical : here a streamlet

there a mere   or mere idea :
the last trail walked on the last day

(his boot on *that* rock? or *this* one?)

'We will find nothing else'

'We will need nothing else'

Parts of the only world there is

'WHAT SORT OF HUMAN FEELING IS IT THAT LOVES A STONE FOR A STONE'S SAKE, AND A CLOUD'S FOR A CLOUD'S'

Green needles carpeting over brown
means walking through dead and dying trees :
red-light gall on an aspen leaf, oyster mushrooms
fallen logs, boots almost silent, a death-soft trail
And how many orchids so far?

Wading knee-deep at the second crossing :
numb at first step (June) or not till the far bank
(mid July), trout darting between your feet
—so stumble and splash—then sunlight
picking out patterns of shattered rock

pyramiding along the crest. Trees up the couloirs
following water, or swarming around the outcrops
topping the ridgeline, opposite slope, and
whaddaya think? 70? 80% dead?
Mouse-ear chickweed, last week's senecio

and some kind of bush—*not ninebark, maybe twobark*
We laugh, and then twinflower, scarlet gilia
(this little penstemon, what's it called?
misty, right) and what I mean by *twinflower*
is vast groves, four inches high

climbing the bank through arnica, bog orchids
aspen, thrush song, louseworts, and spotted coral root
—a forest of spotted coral root—
hemlock, sweet cicely, thousands of columbines
and, as we say, *a pretty little death camas,* a knot

in the crisscross action of time and space :
snow-shattered trees in the upper reaches
a feeling of walking outside my own head
nothing in all the sky but light : a mountain malady
of which no sane person would wish

to be cured : no summit, no goal, just
streams at their sources, *grammar of now*
And pain—faint in the body's ranges—
is it absence or presence? Near or far? One foot
in front of the other foot, crossing the force

of stunted bristlecone, dead below and live above
the point of damage, blunt force
of a narrow, local, long-ago slide of snow—
is that what we carry or what we find? Can't say
I can find the difference : sitting in saxifrage

fringed penstemon, cloud penstemon
—though I think I may have made that one up—
buttercups, many-phlowered phlox, wild parsley/wild carrot
more of that chickweed and at least three kinds
of Indian paintbrush, one blood-red—my totem—

memorizing the slope like a book I know
will burn. And then
we're headed downhill through the stream again
our boots, as always, rearranging rock
all by necessity *lookers-down*

to keep from stumbling, keep from falling
—gravity never takes a day off—
all the way down to that cobble, split
—mid-trail, mid-slope, mid-afternoon—
its oxidized heart a mellow orange

rough gray skin with protruding veins
of quartz, white : I love to touch it
hate to leave it, though now we're hurrying—
Look at that! Ten thousand feet of
pyro cumulus—white-gray-orange on a clear blue sky—

maybe blooming north of here, or maybe between
our truck and *down*, our truck and *out*
—if there is an *out* anywhere inside
this *in*, this Way, this up-in-smoke biography
of steep / rock / snow / leg / go

And those old trees in the avalanche path
—the big one, the famous one—
knocked up-hill where the snow ran down-hill
filled the gorge, ran up the opposite slope :
still there, still silver, piled in sun

among the dark, the live, while up at the source
—on the south-facing, walkable, easy path—
knocked-over aspen still growing
knocked-over spruce still putting out
those tight, tiny, purple cones—

any melody
played for thirty seconds, then let go.

ARCH

n. architectural term: a material curve sustained by gravity
as rapture by grief

—IAN HAMILTON FINLAY

ARCH

of my foot
bruised on the day it

'set out to acquire
a mountain'

the *how*, not rock
that holds it

guesses the pitch
to gather its inch, these

terrible objects
steps collected

on calm summer path
of the avalanche—

eggs of the pipit
sheep bones, eager

to 'lay the forms
of passing clouds'

to introduce
a sea distance

touch each other
in so few points

boot soles / hand holds
groove in the rock by

pebble in the rock by
water—

to suffer the water
beyond all dread

'striking the turf
where first it falls

like a hatchet'
a most unfashionable

projection—bit
which I broke

from the edge of the cliff
bit which the edge

of the cliff broke
from me—mere joint?

or fault stained yellow,
red

this highest lake
no more

than a willow bog
—not *willow bog* but

'widowbirds
have no need

of complex nests'
of walking barefoot

toward the snowfield
(nothing important

has happened yet)
bluebells and bistort

bistort and thistle
'a marvelous stairway

from strength to strength'
in 'the action of resting

one's whole weight
on one leg for about

a minute'
one hundred minutes

between this lake
and the ridge

wind-scoured
the bighorn ram

who stands on the step
of nothing is un-

concerned, 'for the power
of rightly striking the edge

comes only by time
and practice'

(that fucking mud-hole
where my truck

slammed in-
to an aspen tree)

—not *aspen tree* but
'arithmeticians

come to subdue
the mountain'

'pandits
walked two-thousand

steps to the mile'
'a ram's head weighs more

than fifty pounds'
and 'rough fracture

is to be the law
of existence'

its summer path
a steep river

of nailwort, sandwort
forget-me-not, an

eddy-pool
in the lee of a rock

a stonecrop, tart
and yellow—words

like sketching a kind
of larceny

a rock in a pocket
plucked from ten

square miles of folded
strata

its harsh but egal-
itarian light

enlisted
'for you will be helped

by noticing'
that cracks in the stone

are little ravines
that most of the gear

is ex-army
'jettisoned

without great loss'
—as chalk cliffs

by the wearing sea
as plumb-line hung

from a precipice
and 'the Unknown's most

implacable foe'
the foot, 'shod

with protruding spikes'
and drawn to a good

squabble—

UNFINISHED MOUNTAINS

No farther than the first meadow
Not much higher than the second crossing
To the top of the pass, but not the peak
The shelf trail, but not the lake
The highest lake, but not the needles
Circle path in view of the cliffs
Turned back by snow
Blown flat by wind
Pinball gravel and sliding scree
A bad boot, a lost glove
Flat tire, headache, dog with a face full of porcupine
Or lost in timber, low on water
Looking for someplace to cross the river
Waiting out rain in a cave of grand-daddy spruces
Once or twice, the wrong ridge
Once or twice, the wrong map
And one long-remembered day
when the horse fell under me—
we spun downhill on slab rock fifty feet
fetched up in a raspberry patch with bloody noses
Often, thunder
Once, a bear cub
up where the beaver ponds used to be
Hail storm at timberline
Falling rock
And not every hour is malleable
'Ten steps, then stop to breathe'
'three steps, then stop to breathe'
are points on a finite curve.

I HAVE OTHER LIVES

Butt on rock, boots on a spruce
growing straight out over the water, the water

forced, here, through a two-foot channel—
solid rock, cut sometime

in the last million years—
filming a dipper

as it comes near, backs off.
It will fly upstream

or down, but not away :
its habitat is moving water—

cold, white, clear

When I said *high grass* I didn't mean *tall*.
'Go looking for something that frightened you.'
Rocks and willow, rocks and scree,
with 'one cake each of the hard colours'
heavy in the rucksack.
Rucksack when it rhymes with *thick,*
thick because it means *fog,*
ten hundred thousand because it means fog
in a high, far country.

    Not *far country* but fir cone
    Not *fir cone* but firm cnoc
    Not *cnoc* but knack
    Not *knack* but steps
    retracing stoic inscriptions

'Stitching clothes for conscripted soldiers'
'Beacon fires burn for three moons'
'One final assault on the upper bastion'

Oh, and the avalanches
arrayed like so many cannon about to fire.

    Not *fire* but firm
    Not *firm* but arm
    of the hanged man
    swapped for a word
    Not *two* but *one*
    Not *here* but *now,* now

Skirt slides, traverse talus (*vast* the hearts
of flowers among the snows).
Mist pours over the headwall,
follows the same path, knocks me silly
(one deer-track where the rocks tumble).
One deer triggers *wander under,*
under water walk is awkward.
O stand, don't falter, heart
beats hard against a leg's labor :
scissors cut paper, paper wraps rock,
rock balanced on pillar of ice.
And 'the ground moraine does not appear
before the ablation of the tongue.'

    Not *tongue* but trail
    Not *trail* but all
    is positively frightening,
    a fact often misunderstood
    as *hermitscape*   or *heaps of stone*—
    ample opportunity for *calm*

(26 hours, 56 hours
position of paragraphs known by heart)
And 'a large flat piece of rock
wedged in like a volume on a shelf'
bounds, so to speak, down the mountain,
each leg choosing its own course.
In the picturesque or the interregnum
(o immoderate greatness of *vast*), a—

74

'Not big enough to carry much
but he speaks excellent French.'
I turn the page, my
sleep now excellently abridged, see
that Petrarch drew a mountain with a church on top
in the margins of Pliny's *Natural History*
(and fabled, there, with a telescope,
a leathern cup that folded up,
a trail guide opened at random).

I got lost reading *Scramble in the Laps,*
followed all night, so
meadows opened, sparrows opened,
miles and miles of *mirabile dictu,*
sorted out *clast* from *iconoclast*
(interbedded erosion intertongued).
Click here *to sort accident data,*
ascend toward perfectly unobstructed view

of white bistort, black raven,
barbed wire strung round a living tree.
Yarrow stands ready to staunch all wounds
(say proximal conglomerate, distal sand).
Above Swift Creek   (are the others slow?)
checking the knots on the tent fly,
bruise my thumb.

And the whole first day
my horse wouldn't drink from the streams

LEG MUSCLE FINDS A MOUNTAIN
WHERE THE EYE FINDS ONLY THIS OR THAT

Not *this or that* but bobcat scat
I guess—too high for lion

Not *high for lion* but any line
on paper will look like a path

'if you put the dark touch
on the side of it nearest the sun'

Willows have grown at the crossing
—all rock, no tracks to read there

Mountain + water = landscape
or mountain + water = cloud

At Lakes of the Clouds, an empty bottle
flights of fish in the limestone

('thus rigidly to economize the regions of dream')

Say pine-bird, willow-bird
dragging-my-wing-through-the-anthill bird

half a square mile of head-high willow
between me and the trees

Not *the trees* but a stand of white pine
Not *white pine* but the rain we ran from

Not the rain we ran from
but the rain

A GHOST

                  of rock, deceptively whole
                  as a wave is whole

                  at the moment
                  of its breaking

                  'dark with an excess of light'
                  above the trees

                  stopped in the meadow
                  'fingering the white quartz

                  which seamed the granite boulders'
                  an accurate guide

to conduct among the snows
ravens drift

across the ridge-top   dog
or coyote barks in the trees

and 'properly used
danger can have an important meaning'

clear as a stone
on paper   'the pen

should walk slowly
over the ground'

—a task too easily mastered
at altitude

this dead bristlecone, far ridge
quarreling across my line of sight

their 'dark tint passing tenderly'
to boot-on-rock, to stonecrop

a noise half brook, half silence
in the scree   brachiopods

in the limestone, pace
of thought from steep

to steep   a pipit
flies straight up with its wings still, held

by wind
'and with reference to breathing

I do not say what
it is for'

backwards as forwards
long slopes of debris

'rest your hand on a book
so to hold the pen long'

'dressing the action in gallant attire'
(one hat, searched for

on the second day)
the grieving bring a photograph

'made chocolate sherbet
in the summer snow'

not *summer* snow   but summit snow
not summit *snow*   but summit

—it's a verb
trail worn into the white rock

'one had to cross an expanse of sea'
spatter of rain and a gull feather

caught in my jacket zipper
it's far from home   and I

surveying distances
'as if they were your whole estate'

say 'jumped from the top of a cattle car
with his clarinet under his arm'

say 'swam into tarns
to fetch out water lilies'

and there, 'just where the curve
of the petal turns to light'

say 'bloom of the scarlet dye
on shining linen'   strata

of 'utterly harsh and horrible colour'
strata of 'delicate pen lines'   mere

requiring   in crossed branches
bound at the root

a wind is captured, illustrated
by 'syllable of a stammerer'

a stumbler stumbling
up hill from the trail—a boot

                              on rock, a stone
                              in the bristlecone

                    —someone has visited—

                              'guarding the frontier
                              of heaven and earth'

                              elk scat here
                              in the alplily   ants

                              keep rearranging
                              the ashes

                              improbable slip
                              masquerading

as possible   granite
drifting across basalt

(my footprints drying behind me)
rolling on landwave

rock-drunk
sprawled where a siskin

talks in the undertow
'to pause within a hair's breadth

of any appointed mark'
and see

nothing   a kestrel

hangs where east meets west
the ridge

in both directions
concealing force

and 'no series
without a snap somewhere'

OTHER LIVES

AN OLD SCAT FULL OF RED FUR

How old is the song called 'The Wars Are Not Over?'
Black letter, white letter, flimsy sheets
And yet you may see by them how the wind sits
Which you may not do by tossing up a stone
Climbers indulging in rock talk
'Smart money's on that cloud to freeze our tits off'
Bats swallows bats swallows—no moment unguarded
As the guy on the radio said last night
'Let's have "The Pain in My Heart"
And then we'll have the rest of it'
Log clawed open by a black bear
Human footprint in sand called *Sand*
(Walked with their feet, warred with their arms)
And here at the edge of the first snowfield
Devices of concatenation
Bar the way weeping and *weeping their voices rise*
Which means wet socks, a willow thicket
Its branches all entangled with the view
'Show the camel's hair and the colour in it'
Snow in the gullies by the hundreds of tons
Toss up a stone if you want to
A war south of the Great Wall
A white 'strangely delicious'
By which I mean 'sparrow song'
By which I mean 'expression of facts'
And 'the most tender distances of sky'

EXPRESSION OF FACTS

On maps, some trails appear as roads
Snow fields melt before winter, glaciers not
'The aspen leaf in autumn matches the blackbird's eye'
This is not the place to discuss technique
Thomas Hardy called open spaces *ballast*
The crest of the range is seabed
Cape Wrath does not mean *wrath*, but *turning point*
And at every switchback, the view changes
Famous teas come from high mountains
In old photos the slopes are treeless
cut and burned down to their skins
Han Shan wrote his poems on rocks and trees
Li Bai got his songs off cabaret girls from the mountains
It is possible to read by moonlight, but not possible to see color
This snow will melt before morning
When they found Mallory's body
everything in his pockets was readable
Oshá will cure you, hemlock will kill you
In some boulder fields you can stand in dust
and listen to rivers under your feet
'Armies climb riverbanks'
For winter grass the mountain sheep is wholly dependent on wind
In every country wrens are noisy
Thoreau was a pencil-maker's son

I FOUND THIS PENCIL IN A PARKING LOT

I found this pencil in a parking lot
Tree branch lying on a frozen lake

'Not only the world around, but the world around that'

Barbed wire strung through the beet fields
By *classic, heroic nudity* our life was cheered

Headwall, Fluted Peak : in the hard stare, the sweet

Good-looking soldier in helmet and shades
Anything can speak as a riddle, but he looks bored

How many hours guarding their shining oxen?

You and I were drinking tea aged in a tangerine
Not in a tangerine, but in its skin

Where, then, is the sweet fruit?

49 days of spirit-wander
Pack horse tangled in the prayer flags

'What mountain is this, my dear?'

Where there is mountain, something is flat
I found this pencil in a parking lot

DO NOT PRAISE MOST WHAT YOU THINK FEWEST PEOPLE HAVE SEEN

Lion crouched over a dead deer
stares for a moment   before it runs:

snowy pines in the nearly-night
their long shadows tossing the path

Tea masters
call boiling water *wild*

BALLAST

Row of boulders at the glacier's edge
'Darwin turns his horse inland'
as I was counting the 580th step

Red, bare, too steep for snow
the presence of, say,
a cataract notwithstanding

Boot-leather, lichen, elk scat
and 'that most heart-exciting of earthly things'
a broken lace

Kataskapos—the looker down—
'discovered a shattered vertebra
in a small piece of chalk'

Spirit gallops into miles of space
'We hold the reins / at the river bank'

THE MOUNTAINS FLEW OVER THE WATER AS BIRDS

Wander out in the morning with a cup in my hand
A lion scat and three bloody tracks in the driveway
This form of silence called *ellipsis of battle*
And on horsemint salient: a small trouble of wet socks
A yellow flower I can't name
Whistle three bars to cut the gravity
Gravity means: a bullet travels in a line that curves
As the planet curves, and then a little more
'Outflank the second hostile position'
(squirrel runs up the window screen)
'I can't convey how much my boots delighted me'
(sliding down scree fields, fording wet willows
holding my walking stick over my head
as a soldier holds his gun)
'I remember you at Austerlitz! I remember you with the flag!'
(an old corduroy of saplings under the mud)
'Andy carried Stevens in the Sunni Triangle'
'Joey had Marvell stuck in his head'
And what would the gardener say to the untrimmed path?
Pity for the anteater, not the ant
So let's say *ignorant plowboy* if we can't say *motherfucker*
Let's practice adaptive stillness:
A single flight feather merged with rock
25,000 feathers on a large bird
No thoughts, counting seven paces
The mountains flew over the water as birds

ROCKFALL ON A CLIFF HIDDEN BY TREES

Both *arrow* and *laugh* contain *bamboo*
(ink-stick melts on a disc of stone)
Brush or boot, step or pause:
At every switchback the view changes
Toe-hold, hand-hold, short nervous line
'Of quartz in rock at the wrack-line'
For quartz in rock at the wrack-line
Use Chinese-white, well ground, instead of water
(though 'mention of distant places
implies military adventure')
Wealth and ruin   one foot apart:
A locked gate   a missed step
Snow in the gullies by the hundreds of tons
Trail on the far side rimmed with ice
'You will see it reflects the objects beyond it
as in a little black rippled pond'
(where a trout jumps and a fly dies)
A trout jumps and a fly dies
'With other views of the horrid kind'
With views entirely of the horrid kind
A close-up painting of warriors on blood-stained heather
(butterflies apparently licking salt)
'Or have I quietly assumed that we saw everything?'
A trail at morning, the merest it was
Set on quaint grounds of barred colour
like bearings on a shield
A trail at morning, the merest 'it was'
Rockfall, on a cliff hidden by trees

THE STONES OF TAMBURLAINE'S ARMY

No end to it   this 'desperate fidelity'
hills and rivers
'dragged onto the map of war'

as 'every translator gallops off
on a horse of his own devising.'
But here's the story:

Timur the Lame
on his way to war in China
ordered each man to add one stone

to a cairn on the Santash Pass.
And on the way home, each man
to *remove* one stone

from the cairn on the Santash Pass.
And thus could be counted the dead,
you see, by counting the stones that remained.

From this red ridge, I count six mountains
each with its piles of stone:
Tijeras Peak—the Crown—

and Prisoner Peak, and Music,
Marble, Blueberry, Snow:
the trail descending in both directions

massifs dissolving into sand—
Sand Creek—running south
then west to the setting sun.

Lovely, that.
'And even if you were no soldier
you too would weep'

at my translation   of *Pico Aislado*—
not *prisoner*   says my dictionary
and not   *refugee*,

but *isolated, remote, cut off,*
scattered—
                          'No likeness to
that human world below.'

LINES CALLED MAP ARE DIFFERENT
FROM LINES CALLED SONG

LINES CALLED MAP ARE DIFFERENT FROM LINES CALLED
SONG

I said I was climbing, but your eye moves down

I SAID I WAS CLIMBING BUT YOUR EYE MOVES DOWN

'The little streams, transparent though they be'

THE LITTLE STREAMS, TRANSPARENT THOUGH THEY BE

Study Rembrandt's light as it falls on skin

STUDY REMBRANDT'S LIGHT AS IT FALLS ON SKIN

Catastrophe unfinished till the actors bow

CATASTROPHE UNFINISHED TILL THE ACTORS BOW

On Napoleon's road, or the Tea Road

ON NAPOLEON'S ROAD, OR THE TEA ROAD

Dead horse lies at the foot of the gorge

DEAD HORSE LIES AT THE FOOT OF THE GORGE

Pseudo-replication of a single song

PSEUDO-REPLICATION OF A SINGLE SONG

I found a songbird's nest in the mouth of a cannon

I FOUND A SONGBIRD'S NEST IN THE MOUTH OF A
CANNON

Method of transport over the mountains

METHOD OF TRANSPORT OVER THE MOUNTAINS

Place barrel of the cannon into a hollowed tree

PLACE BARREL OF THE CANNON INTO A HOLLOWED TREE

Halfway up a thousand-foot slope, digging my foot out of snow

HALFWAY UP A THOUSAND-FOOT SLOPE, DIGGING MY
FOOT OUT OF SNOW

'This loss of professional distance only lasted about ten minutes'

THIS LOSS OF PROFESSIONAL DISTANCE ONLY LASTED
ABOUT TEN MINUTES

Five years from powder snow to *firn* snow to ice

FIVE YEARS FROM POWDER SNOW TO *FIRN* SNOW TO ICE

It's morning; let sun hit the mirror

IT'S MORNING; LET SUN HIT THE MIRROR

'A morning painfully spent in balancing phrases'

A MORNING PAINFULLY SPENT IN BALANCING PHRASES

'I don't know what they attacked; I don't know what they assumed
    they attacked'

I DON'T KNOW WHAT THEY ATTACKED;
I DON'T KNOW WHAT THEY ASSUMED THEY ATTACKED

Pull the mare's head into your lap

PULL THE MARE'S HEAD INTO YOUR LAP

Sit for an hour with a cocked pistol

SIT FOR AN HOUR WITH A COCKED PISTOL

Glaciers divided from the high snows

GLACIERS DIVIDED FROM THE HIGH SNOWS

Lines called map are different from lines called song

'Wind and thunder cross my threshold'
Child masturbating on the edge of a door
—any moment in which to practice *calm*
'With your own body carry yourself'
Though we were less strong
than stubborn
Writing with gloves on, burning scrap
Freeing a doe with her hind leg caught in a fence
'If you don't wash your clothes
you can carry smoke'
scribbled inside my copy of *High Path*
'Roads appear and disappear'
'We walk'd upon the very brink'
Large, therefore, is spoken of
Tea settles in a dirty cup
And a few pennies left
for the news:
'War Horses Graze by the City Walls'
'Seed Pods Ripen to Brilliant Red'
Trim the wicks, so the lamps burn brighter
Leave the window open
for company
The car high-centered in knee-deep ruts
Ridge-tops shining by starlight
As the master says: impossible
to set a mountain before your eyes

Murray wrote *Mountaineering in Scotland*
in a German P.O.W. camp
(clothes drying in the open air)
and 'not merely to divide the light
behind some human figure'
And not merely to divide the light
did Gwen Moffat go on her climbing spree:
Holly Tree, Snowden
and six Welsh peaks I can't pronounce
Barefoot on granite, AWOL in 1945
(watercress green on the cliff-tops)
To wander is Daoist code for ecstasy

To wander is code for ecstasy:
'lodging in damp rhododendron beds
storm-beaten, stupefied, and sulky'
Or laughing, stupefied, and sulky
for nothing is blacker than wet ink
while 'even the darkest part of the mountain
is lighter than white paper'
(sunlight or cloud on vertical rock
blue growing tips of the spruce trees)
Play it with the brush, as Ruskin says
until it finds its place

Play it with the brush till it finds its place
Hillary answered, 'because it's there'
when he got fucking tired of the question
His Sherpas had no word for *summit*
(footprint of the pot in ashes)
Sherpas have no word for *summit*
and 'the Way's been in ruins a thousand years'
Scratch of coarse lead on coarse paper
Clothes drying in the open air
(Push through willows, there's a path here somewhere)
Murray wrote *Mountaineering in Scotland*
in a German P.O.W. camp—twice

That it was carried close to the body
That clearly no mountain was visible
That *Coruisk* and the *Black Cuillin*
Buachaille Etive Mor
Could only be anagram, or code
That food was traded for toilet paper
That envelopes, can labels, homemade ink
That Gneiss is good, Gabbro better
Both 'rough and reliable comrades'
That skirting, that scrambling, that water in the bed
'That we were, in fact, free to select one route'
That magnetic rocks attract the needle
That some flowers are carnivorous
That the very next day cigarettes were traded
For a stump of very bad pencil
That axe, that compass, that cloud, that fire
Escape routes real   and imagined
'Cluttered with incoherent snow'
That eight hundred feet, twelve hundred feet
That tall pines and sun-drenched moor
'Of which, most sadly, we had time to read
But one chapter and that quickly'
That weary arm hews black ice
That breeches in tatters, coil of rope
Boot nails in a state of decrepitude
That hills are said to repay trust—
The fells, the flanks, the wings, the waves—
Each single harebell blooming
On its wind-adapted stem

AS MOVING WATER TO A MOUNTAIN

Writing is a discipline of reading, and reading a discipline of writing. To materialize this dialectic, the poems make extensive use of borrowed language from sources named in these notes. Not all borrowings are typographically distinguished in the text, and some marked text is not sampled. I apologize for unintentional omissions in the following.

Paths to this book began at Hawthornden Castle in 2002, when Tom Pow introduced me to Simon Schama's *Landscape and Memory*. In the same month, I found at the Scottish Poetry Library two titles in the Pocketbook series from Alec Finlay's Morning Star Editions: *The Way to Cold Mountain: a Scottish mountains anthology* and Hamish Fulton's *Wild Life: walks in the Cairngorms*. All these pushed me to older European accounts of mountains, to Rebecca Solnit's *Wanderlust: A History of Walking,* and deeper into John Ruskin, particularly *Elements of Drawing* and *Modern Painters IV: On Mountain Beauty.* Soon after, as the poems I was writing moved closer to home, it was Robert Macfarlane's *Mountains of the Mind* that clarified my subject; like Ruskin's, his became a voice to which the poems returned and returned, like birds to their native cliffs.

Among Scottish mountaineering classics, Nan Shepherd's *The Living Mountain,* W.H. Murray's *Mountaineering in Scotland,* and David Craig's *Native Stones* all prove porous to Daoist and Buddhist thought. Translators of Chinese mountain poetry give uneven access to that tradition. For fragments of image, world, and word, I am indebted to translations and commentary by A.C. Graham, Arthur Cooper, and David Hinton, while Yunte Huang's *Shi: A Radical Reading of Chinese Poetry* and Francois Cheng's *Chinese Poetic Writing* supplied a more refracted, less Englished glimpse of Chinese grammar as a script *of* and *for* perception. Many thanks to Arthur Sze, for pointing me toward some of these sources.

A Tree at Its Birthplace / A Boulder at Its Resting Place; *A Walk Is a Fact for the Walker and Fiction for Everyone Else*; and *No Thoughts, Counting Seven Paces* are works by walking artist Hamish Fulton . . . though it was Richard Long who walked the spiral.

'Not by Scale but by Aggregation' is Ruskin, from *On Mountain Beauty*.

'In Country that Is Rough, but Not Difficult . . . ' and 'The One That Feeds It and the One that Drains It . . . ' are Nan Shepherd, from *The Living Mountain*.

'Beyond Temporary, Like Snow Flurry' is from Tory Dent's "RIP, My Love," in *HIV, Mon Amor*.

'To Have Pain Is to Have Certainty, To Hear of Pain Is to Have Doubt' is Elaine Scarry, from *The Body in Pain*.

'Without Exaggeration, without Mystery, without Enmity, and without Mercy' is Ruskin's praise of Byron, a poet 'who spoke only of what he had seen'—unlike Wordsworth, whose intimations of immortality Ruskin found 'idle.'

'What Sort of Human Feeling Is It that Loves a Stone . . . ' is also proposed in contrast to Wordsworth's tendency to regard nature as his looking glass. Both are from Ruskin's autobiography, *Praeterita*.

Lines quoted at the end of 'Days Grow Shorter but the Trails Do Not' are from Brian Teare's "It is hard to realize at the time of helplessness that that is the time to be awake and aware," in *The Empty Form Goes All the Way to Heaven*.

'Sea Foam, for Instance, Cannot Be Drawn at All' is Ruskin in *The Elements of Drawing*. *A tract of solitude and savageness* was the first published definition of *wilderness*, in Samuel Johnson's 1755 dictionary.

"Lost" begins with a line from Arthur Cooper's translation of one of Li Bai's last poems, and ends with David Craig's critique of W.H. Murray's lifelong longing for transcendence.

Terrible objects was Edmund Burke's phrase for objects, views, encounters—*things*—that evoke the peculiar blend of pleasure and terror he called *Sublime*.

"The Mountains Flew Over the Water as Birds" uses language from Elizabeth Samet's *Soldier's Heart: Reading Literature through Peace and War at West Point*.

"The Stones of Tamburlaine's Army" gleans from translations in C.H. Kwock & Vincent McHugh's *Old Friend from Far Away*.

More years ago than I care to say, the artist Suzanne Theodora White taught me to look on the light in Rembrandt's *Self-Portrait as an Old Man* as an ethical act.

Loch Coruisk (CORushk) (Sc. GAELIC: *Coire Uisg*: kettle of water) is a freshwater loch at the foot of the Black Cuillin (COOLun) (Sc. GAELIC: *Cuileann*: holly), a mountain range on the Isle of Skye. Buachaille Étive Mór ([BOOuchEELyuh ET-CHiv MOR *or* Etie MOR) (Sc. GAELIC: great herdsman of Etive) is a mountain near Glen Coe. All three are iconic locations of the Scottish Highlands and Islands.

Not this, but that constructions are adapted from Alec Finlay's *credos*, which were, in turn, adapted from Stevie Smith's "Not Waving, but Drowning."

Hyphenated compounds are adapted, or adopted, from Yunte Huang's translations of Chinese radicals.

Further sources that shaped the book—many of which are quoted, paraphrased, or shadowed in the text—include Michael O'Hanlon: *The Colorado Sangre de Cristo: A Complete Trail Guide*; U.S. Geological Survey: *The Geologic Story of Colorado's Sangre de Cristo Mountains*; Wayne Anderson: *Geology of the Custer County Area, South-Central Colorado*; Jack Reed & Gene Ellis: *Rocks Above the Clouds: A Climber's Guide to Colorado Mountain Geology*; Wilhelm Paulcke & Helmut Dumler: *Hazards in Mountaineering*; Leslie Stephen: *The Playground of Europe*; Gwen Moffat: *Space Below My Feet*; Marjorie Hope Nicolson: *Mountain Gloom and Mountain Glory: The Development of the Aesthetics of the Infinite*; and Dominique T. Pasqualini: *The Time of Tea*. Other texts sampled (or, in some cases, mangled) include Andy Russell: *Horns in the High Country*; Edward Whymper: *Scrambles*

Amongst the Alps; John Dennis's 1688 letters from the Alps, qtd by Macfarlane; Samuel Johnson: *A Journey to the Western Islands of Scotland*, qtd by everybody; W.G. Sebald: *Vertigo*; Leo Tolstoy: *War and Peace*. Lines in several poems—most notably "What Sort of Human Feeling . . . "—owe their lives to Teresa & Doug Cain, whose words-while-walking lodge in my notebooks and ghost my recordings of streams and wind. Other companions haunting these paths include some notable four-leggeds: Spook, José, Rennie, Bon, Abbey, Nimbus, Angel, & Babe.

Because this book was written over many years—sharing space and time with three other books published before it—it is impossible to thank everyone whose critical attention contributed to its evolution: my gratitude resides in the poems. Lesley Smith—who misses neither a wayward word nor the most far-traveled allusion—was, once again, my book's most constant friend. With Brian Teare I shared commitment to embodiment, a pact against the silencing of pain. I am grateful for what his friendship brought to the book, and for what he cut out of it. I also extend sincerest thanks to the doctors, physical therapists, massage therapists, and pharmacists, who, for so many decades, have made it possible for my injured and hyper-reactive body to cross oceans and move through mountains. First and last, I thank Janet Holmes, true friend not only to poetry, but to poets.

"And Just for the Record, I'd Like to Say that I Can't Do What I Just Did" & "Days Grow Shorter but the Trails Do Not" are for Gary & Laura Faulkenberry, & for Teresa & Doug Cain, Horn Lakes, September 2015.

"Pockets of Detail, Unsurrounded" is in memory of Nimbus and of Angel.

"Long Walk after Too Little Sleep" is for my brother, Joe, who stayed in camp, Huérfano Basin, July 2007.

"On a Narrow, Side-Hill, Excuse for a Trail," "Small Volcano of a Mushroom, Pushing through Soil" & "I Have Other Lives" are for T&D, North Taylor Creek, July 2015.

"What Sort of Human Feeling Is It that Loves a Stone . . . " is for T&D, 10 July 2016, anniversary of Michael's fall and the day the Hayden Pass Fire blew up.

"Blue Tin Cup" & "Lost" are in memory of Michael. "Tent Book" is in memory of Michael & of Nimbus.

"Ghost" is for all companions, Music Pass & beyond, 2002–2012.

"I Found This Pencil in a Parking Lot" is for Peggy Yocom, who knows why we must ask *what mountain.*

"Expression of Facts" is for Mick & Monica Backsen, the factish ones.

"That Most Heart-Exciting of Earthly Things" is for Lisa Kaufman, 1987.

"Because It Was a Mountain Where I Fell," "To Have Pain Is to Have Certainty," & poems that follow are for my foot, hip, spine, and pelvis, Chipita Peak, June 1981.

Rock teas
are Chinese oolongs
cultivated for a thousand years
in the granite-rich soils
of Wuyi Mountain,
Fujian Province
: :
sip phantom mountain
every morning in exile

ACKNOWLEDGMENTS

Many thanks to the editors & staff of journals who first published some of these poems, sometimes in different versions—

Beloit Poetry Journal for "A Ghost," & "That Most Heart-Exciting of Earthly Things"

Cerise Press for "An Old Scat Full of Red Fur," "Ballast," & "Murray Wrote *Mountaineering in Scotland*"

Clade Song for "Pockets of Detail, Unsurrounded," & "Small Volcano of a Mushroom, Pushing Through Soil"

Colorado Review for "I Found This Pencil in a Parking Lot"

Copper Nickel for "Another Haunting, the Pencil Line"

Free Verse for "After Paradise," "Alive," "Leg Muscle Finds a Mountain Where the Eye Finds Only This or That," "Beyond Temporary, Like Snow Flurry," "Of Half the Views I Have Yet Said Nothing," "Expression of Facts," & "The Stones of Tamburlaine's Army"

The Missouri Review On Line for "A Walk Is Fact for the Walker and Fiction for Everyone Else"

iO for "Lines Called Map Are Different from Lines Called Song"

Plumwood Mountain: An Australian Journal of Ecopoetry & Ecopoetics for "Route Sketched on a Map, As If Walking," & "In Country That Is Rough but Not Difficult, One Sees Where One Is and Where One Is Going at the Same Time"

Spacecraft Projects for "At a Rockfall Ending in Willow, A Larkspur Taller than Willow," "Tent Book," "The Mountains Flew Over the Water as Birds," & "Rockfall on a Cliff Hidden by Trees"

Terrain.org: A Journal of the Built + Natural Environments for "In the 15th Chapter on Infinity, Try to Arrest One Detail"

The Tupelo Quarterly for "To Speak of One Is to Speak of the Other," which also appeared as a Tupelo Press broadside.

"Murray Wrote *Mountaineering in Scotland*" may also be glimpsed at Elgol, Isle of Skye, as part of Alec Finlay's online *Còmhlan Bheanntan / A Company of Mountains.*

Warm thanks, also, to The Bothy Project, Scotland, for a residency at Sweeney's Bothy, Isle of Eigg; to Hawthornden International Writers Retreat, for a month at Hawthornden Castle; to the Ruskin Library, University of Lancaster, for access to Ruskin's drawings and geology notebooks; and to George Mason University, for sabbatical time to begin this book . . . and then, again, to finish it.

ABOUT THE AUTHOR

SUSAN TICHY is the author of three previous books from Ahsahta—*Trafficke* (2015), *Gallowglass* (2010), and *Bone Pagoda* (2007)—as well as *A Smell of Burning Starts the Day* and *The Hands in Exile,* a National Poetry Series selection. Her poems, collaborations, and mixed-genre works have been published in the U.S., Britain, and Australia, and recognized by numerous awards, including a fellowship from the National Endowment for the Arts. In 2019 she retires from 30 years teaching in the MFA and BFA programs at George Mason University. Except when teaching, she has lived for thirty-six years in the foothills of the Wet Mountains/Sierra Mojada, in a cabin she and her late husband built by hand. West of her cabin lies an 80-mile chain of peaks and ridges with ten summits over 14,000 feet: the Colorado Sangre de Cristo, a fault-block uplift range on whose momentarily stilled rock most of these poems found life.

AHSAHTA PRESS

NEW SERIES